Dearest Son

Become Who
You Were Created To Be

Jeremy Mark Lane

D1177038

Copyright © 2015 Jeremy Mark Lane

All rights reserved.

ISBN: 1515359603
ISBN-13: 978-1515359609

To the men out there who believe they aren't worth fighting for:

That's a lie. God has fought for you. He continues to fight for you. Give him the next thirty days to battle for your heart and see what happens. It will be more than you ever expected.

To my brothers, who taught me how to battle.

To my wife, who battles alongside me every day.

To Abbie, Allie, and Corbin – I won't ever stop battling on your behalf.

DAY 1

WHERE ARE YOU?

Dearest Son,

Where are you? I called this out to the first man and I call it out to you now. Where are you?

But the Lord God called to the man and said to him, "Where are you?" And he said, "I heard the sound of you in the garden, and I was afraid, because I was naked, and I hid myself." - Genesis 3: 9-10

You hide because your view of Me is incomplete. You view Me as Creator of all you see, Master of Heaven and Earth. You fear Me as the Righteous Judge. Your mind tells you that I am the Lord.
You are correct - I am these things.

I am the God of the Universe.
And God said, "Let there be light," and there was light. - Genesis 1:3

I am the God that builds nations.
And I will make of you a great nation, and I will bless you and make your name great, so that you will be a blessing. - Genesis 12:2

I am the God that tolerates the worship of no other.

Do not turn to idols or make for yourselves any gods of cast metal: I am the LORD your God. - Leviticus 19:4

And I am so much more. Starting right now, I ask that you view me for all that I am.

My dearest son, I am your most Loving Father. You are My son. You do not realize it, but you are the son of the Most High King. You are royalty. I have waited as a patient Father for you to take your rightful place, my son, but I seek to wait no longer. I deeply desire to have a relationship with you. To spend time each day with the child I love so dearly. My heart aches for you. All of the questions you have, I will answer.

But first...I ask again.
Where are you?

Answer, "I am here, Father. I am here."

See what kind of love the Father has given to us, that we should be called children of God; and so we are. - 1 John 3:1

You need not hide from Me ever again, My dearest son. You are loved.

Ask God to reveal all of the reasons you have run from Him over the course of your life. What thoughts, behaviors, or beliefs have sent you into hiding?

_____

_____

_____

_____

_____

_____

_____

_____

_____

_____

_____

_____

_____

_____

_____

_____

_____

_____

_____

_____

_____

_____

_____

_____

_____

_____

_____

_____

PRAYER

Father,

I know, until now, I have spent my life hiding from You. I was afraid. I was naked, exposed, with all of my mistakes and regrets and worries and problems and imperfections on display. I didn't want You to see them. I didn't want You to be disappointed in me. I didn't want to discuss it. I was afraid of Your judgment.

Why would the Creator of all things tolerate my mess? I ran out of fear and shame. I have sought out other idols – things that I thought could bring me happiness, bring me purpose – and I have chased after them. I have captured them and watched them turn to poison in my hands. I have so many questions for You. There are so many things I don't understand.

I thank You for Your patience. And for Your love. I thank you for not giving up on me, though You've seen me at my worst. I realize now that there is no hiding from You. I understand that You know everything about me, and that you still deeply desire to have a relationship with me. To spend time with me every day. I understand that this is love. The love of my Father.

Thank you for who You are. I am here, Father. Amen.

DAY 2

WHAT ARE YOU LOOKING FOR?

Dearest Son,

What are you looking for? What is it that you seek? What is it that you have searched for and that you continue to search for even now?
Why are you unfulfilled?
Why aren't you happy?

You are searching. You plod along on this journey and you look down every side road, hoping to see it. Sometimes a thing or a person or a group of people come along that look so enticing, so perfect, and you take hold of this new thing and your heart is alive for a moment. Then you feel yourself searching again.

Do not turn away after useless idols. They can do you no good, nor can they rescue you, because they are useless. - 1 Samuel 12:21

You can <u>feel</u> this hole inside of you, and your every desire is to <u>fill</u> it. Fill it with anything. With anybody.

That party.
That bar.
Those friends.
That place.
That woman.

That house.
Those kids.
That job.

Son, not only will these things never, ever serve the purpose you are using them for, but they are slowly making you worse. Making you sick. Why?

They exchanged the truth of God for a lie, and worshipped and served created things rather than the Creator - who is forever praised. Amen. - Romans 1:25

You were created to know Me. You were designed for a relationship with Me, your Father. Your heart was crafted in such a way that when you fill it with anything but Me, when you ask anything or anyone else to bring your heart to life, that thing turns to poison. It makes you worse.

My children would save themselves so much time, and so much hurt, if they would accept this one truth: There is no happiness without Me. You will never fully know life without Me. The hole you feel inside of you is there for a reason - and it cannot be filled with anything or anyone but Me.

I love those who love me, and those who seek me find me. - Proverbs 8:17

What are you looking for? You're looking for your Father. And I cannot wait to see you fully alive.

The Lord your God will circumcise your hearts and the hearts of your descendants, so that you may love him with all your heart and with all your soul, **and live.** - Deuteronomy 30:6

Make a list of every person, thing or situation you have looked to for happiness or purpose over the last five years of your life.

_____

_____

_____

_____

_____

_____

_____

_____

_____

_____

_____

_____

_____

_____

_____

_____

_____

_____

_____

_____

_____

_____

_____

_____

_____

_____

_____

_____

_____

_____

_____

_____

PRAYER

Father,

I ask that You forgive me for all of the wasted time I've
spent chasing useless things. You have shown me time and
time again, through my lack of fulfillment, my lack of
purpose, that You are the only one that can fill this hole in
me, yet I struggled against You and continued on my own
way.

I have searched for and taken hold of things that I thought
would bring my heart to life – that would let me really live –
and every time they poison me. They are not You, and they
cannot be what You are. They are useless idols.

I know now that I was created for nothing less than a full,
complete relationship with You. After a lifetime of chasing
useless things, I stand before You now in complete
surrender. You promise that anyone who seeks You will find
You, and from this day forward I will seek You. Show me
love. Show me joy. Show me peace. Show me everything
You want me to see. Above all, show me You. Bring me to
life, Father.

Amen.

DAY 3

WHY DARKNESS?

Dearest Son,

Why are you choosing darkness?

If anyone walks in the day, he does not stumble, because he sees the light of this world. But if anyone walks in the night, he stumbles, because the light is not in him." - John 11: 9-10

The human condition is to walk in darkness. To wander without aim, hoping to stumble upon something that makes your heart wake up. Something that makes you come alive. This is not only wrong, it's dangerous.

The way of the wicked is like deep darkness; they do not know over what they stumble. - Proverbs 4:19

Darkness is the territory of the enemy. He lives there. He lurks there waiting to set his trap, waiting to make My children his slaves. He wants you to be in bondage. To hurt, to worry, and to continue walking in darkness. To stumble.

For we do not wrestle against flesh and blood, but against the rulers, against the authorities, against the cosmic powers over this present darkness, against the spiritual forces of evil in the heavenly places. - Ephesians 3:12

10

Imagine what this does to My heart. Imagine how your Father hurts over this.

I ask you to take the light. Find the light that I have given you and walk in it. Soak it in. Live in it. Be it. Show it to others.

And this is the judgment: the light has come into the world, and people loved the darkness rather than the light because their works were evil. For everyone who does wicked things hates the light and does not come to the light, lest his works should be exposed. But whoever does what is true comes to the light, so that it may be clearly seen that his works have been carried out in God. - John 3: 19-21

You are loved beyond measure. Step into the light. I want to see My son in all his glory.

*Arise, shine, for your **light** has come, and the **glory of God** has risen upon you.* - Isaiah 60:1

Has there been a time when you've asked God to reveal His direction for your life? Ask Him now and write down the answer.

_____

_____

_____

_____

_____

_____

_____

_____

_____

_____

_____

_____

_____

_____

_____

_____

_____

_____

_____

_____

_____

_____

_____

_____

_____

_____

_____

_____

_____

_____

_____

_____

_____

_____

PRAYER

Father,

Please forgive me for choosing darkness over Your light for so long. I stumbled around without direction, falling over things and stepping into traps and falling time after time, and still You walked patiently beside me. You continually called out to me, reached out to me, but I refused Your every effort.

I know now that the darkness I walked in is the worst place a person can be. Darkness is where the enemy is, and it comes from our own closed eyes and our own closed heart. I am sorry that I turned away from You for so long.

Above all things, Father, I thank You for rescuing me from that bondage. I thank You for relentlessly fighting for me and for loving me enough to win me back. You broke the chains of my existence, struck a light in the darkness, and led me out by the hand. You are my rescuer and my redeemer. You are all things.

I ask now God that You give me the light – that your love and freedom burns within me so intensely that it shines like a light to the rest of the world. Help me live, Father. Truly live. Let the glory of God rise upon me. Amen.

DAY 4

IMAGINE

Dearest Son,

Imagine that you stand upon a mountain top that overlooks a great valley. In the valley below there are millions of people, trudging in all possible directions, no destination before them and no goals to reach. No end. They are filthy. They are hungry. They thirst so badly that it causes them physical pain. Metal chains wrap around their necks and trail behind them, attached to massive clumps of rotting garbage, which each person drags to the best of their ability. Some reach the end of their will to exist and crumple down onto the ground. The sight is pitiful. Slaves, all of them.

*For when you were slaves of sin, you were free in regard to righteousness. But what fruit were you getting at that time from the things of which you are now ashamed? For the end of those things **is death.*** – Romans 6:20

Then, you see them. You see your children. Your daughters – princesses relegated to servitude. Their beauty hidden beneath layers of filth, the mark of a slave. Your son, the great prince, walks with his head down watching his own wasted steps. What he should have been now just a fading memory. You are broken at the sight, but your heart tells you that if they would just look up at you, if they would just seek your face

14

their bonds would be broken. They would be free, and clean, and fed. They would drink from life-giving waters. They would be alive again.

Children, please just turn to your Father, you say. Please.

But from there you will seek the Lord your God and you will find him, if you search after him with all your heart and with all your soul. When you are in tribulation, and all these things come upon you in the latter days, you will return to the Lord your God and obey his voice. For the Lord your God is a merciful God. He will not leave you or destroy you or forget the covenant with your fathers that he swore to them. – Deuteronomy 4: 29-31

And they look up at you. And they see your face. And at once you are wrapping your arms around them and covering them in your love.

"How did this happen?"

"We don't know. It just happened. We didn't even realize it until it had already happened."

"Did you defend yourselves?"

"No. We didn't know we were in battle until it was too late."

"You are My children and I love you. Always find your strength in Me, your Father. You are not slaves. You are royalty. Never again will you live in bondage."

Yes, My son, imagine that.

Imagine that.

The LORD looks down from heaven on the children of man, to see if there are any who understand, who seek after God. – Psalm 14:2

Imagine watching the person you love most in the world live their life as a slave. How would that make you feel?

_____
_____
_____
_____
_____
_____
_____
_____
_____
_____
_____
_____
_____
_____
_____
_____
_____
_____
_____
_____
_____
_____
_____
_____
_____

PRAYER

Father,

I am sorry that I have been a slave to sin for so long. I am sorry that I allowed myself to become complacent in my life, and self-sufficient in my mind. It is in this mediocrity that the enemy moves to enslave us. I ask that You forgive me for allowing this to happen.

I promise, from this point forward, I will always keep my eyes turned toward You. I will always remain aware and alert to everything in my life, and measure the fruit of each thing. I will not allow myself to enter bondage again. Your children are not slaves of the enemy. I promise to fight. To battle. To always call out for You.

I will seek after God.

Amen.

DAY 5

IT IS A CHOICE

Dearest Son,

It is a choice.

You can continue in weakness, or you can choose power.

I have given you authority to trample on snakes and scorpions and to overcome all the power of the enemy; nothing will harm you. - Luke 10: 19

You can continue in slavery, or you can choose freedom.

It is for freedom that Christ has set us free. Stand firm, and do not let yourselves be burdened again by a yoke of slavery. - Galatians 5:1

You can continue in frustration, or you can choose joy.

Until now you have not asked for anything in my name. Ask and you will receive, and your joy will be complete. - John 16:24

You can continue existing, or you can choose life.

Even youths grow tired and weary, and young men stumble and fall; but those who hope in the Lord will renew their strength.

They will soar on wings like eagles; they will run and not grow weary, they will walk and not be faint. - Isaiah 40:31

You can continue toward hell, or you can choose heaven.

Then the angel showed me the river of the water of life, as clear as crystal, flowing from the throne of God and of the Lamb down the middle of the great street of the city. On each side of the river stood the tree of life, bearing twelve crops of fruit, yielding its fruit every month. And the leaves of the tree are for the healing of the nations. No longer will there be any curse. The throne of God and of the Lamb will be in the city, and his servants will serve him. They will see his face, and his name will be on their foreheads. There will be no more night. They will not need the light of a lamp or the light of the sun, for the Lord God will give them light. And they will reign for ever and ever.
- Revelation 22:1-5

It is a choice, and it's yours to make.

Think of and list specific situations or times in your life when you feel that you chose the opposite of what God wanted for you.

_____

_____

_____

_____

_____

_____

_____

_____

_____

_____

_____

_____

_____

_____

_____

_____

_____

_____

_____

_____

_____

_____

_____

_____

_____

_____

_____

_____

_____

_____

PRAYER

Father,

I ask that You forgive me for my years of walking in weakness. I thought I had power, I thought I was self-sufficient. I thought I had control. But what I had was nothing. Without You, there is nothing but weakness.

Forgive me for choosing to continue in slavery. I pulled myself along, with my head down, for so many years before finally listening to Your call. I was in bondage and a slave to the world.

Forgive me for wallowing in frustration for so long. For wondering why, despite my very best efforts, nothing seemed to work out the way it was supposed to. I would allow my frustration to spill onto those I love the most.

Forgive me for just existing. For just making it through each day, and not seeing Your hand in my life every minute of every day. I was alive, but was not living.

Starting now, I choose power over weakness. I choose freedom over slavery. I choose joy over frustration. Most of all, I choose to live. I choose You, Father.

Amen.

DAY 6

PRISONER OF WAR

Prisoner: a person captured and kept confined by an opponent, enemy, or criminal.

Dearest Son,

There is a war taking place right now. It's all around you, and very few are even aware that it's happening. Yet, every person - every last person on earth - is a prisoner of it.

War: a struggle or conflict between opposing forces for a particular end

You are all prisoners of war.

What makes this war different, however, is that the prisoners CHOOSE what side they will serve. They choose whom they will be captive to.

Captive: owned and controlled by another and operated for its needs

The choices in this battle are clear - become captive to the Lord your God, or captive to the enemy. Captive to Light, or to darkness. Life, or death. You must choose God. To remain idle, to do nothing, is to choose the enemy. Things in the dark are most dangerous to those who don't know they are in it.

The results of the choice are just as clear - those who become prisoner to the enemy will struggle and stumble through their existence, consumed by meaningless things, always struggling against their own bondage. Never free, never alive.

Bondage: servitude or subjugation to a controlling person or force

Those who choose God will come fully into what and who they were created to be. They will understand and begin to strive after their own full potential, which is more than they ever could have imagined. They will feel their hearts restored and their vision cleared. They will stand straight, fully alive, and begin walking the path of their own purpose. They are fueled by power and joy. By becoming prisoner to God, they become free.

Free: relieved from or lacking something and especially something unpleasant or burdensome
Free: not subject to restriction or official control
Free: not obstructed, restricted, or impeded
Free: capable of moving or turning in any direction
Free: not costing or charging anything
Free: not restricted by or conforming to conventional forms
Free: not allowing slavery

All are prisoners. Many are missing in action. But none are forgotten. Choose your Father.

The Spirit of the Sovereign Lord is on me, because the Lord has anointed me to proclaim the good news to the poor. He has sent me to bind up the brokenhearted, to proclaim freedom for the captives and release from darkness for the prisoners. - Isaiah 61:1

How do you feel your life would be different if you were free from everything that hinders you?

_____

_____

_____

_____

_____

_____

_____

_____

_____

_____

_____

_____

_____

_____

_____

_____

_____

_____

_____

_____

_____

_____

_____

_____

_____

_____

_____

_____

_____

_____

_____

_____

PRAYER

Father,

I will no longer be a prisoner to the enemy in this war. I feel the combat, and I understand the battle, and I will not lose my freedom to the opponent.

I present myself as Your captive – captive never again to darkness, idleness, and death, but to the light You provide, the abundant life You offer, and the eternity You promise.

Strengthen me, Father, to avoid the distraction of meaningless things. Empower me to avoid slavery to the things of this world, and instead to pour all of my time, energy, and heart into things of You.

Make me into what and who You created me to be. Clear my vision, clean and restore my heart, and push me into my full potential. Raise me up, straighten my path, and guide my steps, Father. Fuel me with Your power and Your joy and Your purpose. Bring me fully to life.

In being captive to You I claim my freedom. Bind up my heart, Lord. Declare my freedom and release me from darkness.

Amen.

DAY 7

BELT OF TRUTH

Dearest Son,

Stand firm then, with the belt of truth buckled around your waist... - Ephesians 6:14

Truth is the only defense against one of the enemy's greatest weapons - his lies. He hates your freedom, and is livid at your victories, and will waste no time in filling your mind with lies and doubt about who you are, what you've done, and what I have for your future.

Lie: Jesus doesn't save you.

TRUTH*: Jesus answered, "I am the way and the truth and the life. No one comes to the Father except through me.* - John 14:6

Lie: God doesn't give guidance.

TRUTH: *But when he, the Spirit of truth, comes, he will guide you into all the truth. He will not speak on his own; he will speak only what he hears, and he will tell you what is yet to come.* - John 16:13

Lie: God doesn't hear you.

TRUTH*: The LORD is near to all who call on him, to all who call on him in truth.* - Psalm 145:18

Lie: You must be better. You must clean up your act before God will pay attention to you.

TRUTH*: For the law was given through Moses; grace and truth came through Jesus Christ.* - John 1:17

Lie: This excitement will wear off soon.

TRUTH*: because of the truth, which lives in us and will be with us forever.* - 2 John 1:2

Battle each lie with truth and you cannot be defeated.

What do you believe is the most powerful lie the enemy is using against you right now?

_____

_____

_____

_____

_____

_____

_____

_____

_____

_____

_____

_____

_____

_____

_____

_____

_____

_____

_____

_____

_____

_____

_____

_____

_____

_____

_____

_____

_____

PRAYER

Father,

I know that this battle is ongoing. I know that the enemy will never stop coming after me, will never stop his attacks on my heart and mind. I also know that You will never stop battling on my behalf, and that You are always with me no matter the circumstance.

I ask today and every day that you wrap me fully in your armor. It is only with Your protection that I can stand against his schemes. Place Your belt of truth around my waist, Father, and give me the ability to distinguish truth from a lie, good from evil.

The truth is that no matter what I've done, what mistakes I've made, or how many lies I've believed – I am a child of God and my purpose and my future lie in You. You hold all of it in Your hands. You save, You redeem, You hear us, and You fight on our behalf. This is truth.

Equip and strengthen me to battle lies with truth, Father.

Amen.

DAY 8

BREASTPLATE OF RIGHTEOUSNESS

Dearest Son,

Don't stop battling.

It is inevitable that, at some point, one of the enemy's blows will get past your defenses. You will be caught unaware and a thought, a reaction, a feeling will be upon you that is not of Me. The enemy will strike for your heart, but if you are covered in my armor, the blow will glance off your breastplate without effect.

With the breastplate of righteousness in place... - Ephesians 6:14

Without this breastplate, without righteousness, the enemy's blows would be fatal. With it, you are protected.

Wealth is worthless in the day of wrath, but righteousness delivers from death. - Proverbs 11:4

But it is not your own righteousness that will protect you - without Me, you have none.

All of us have become like one who is unclean, and all our righteous acts are like filthy rags; we all shrivel up like a leaf, and like the wind our sins sweep us away. - Isaiah 64:6

It is only My righteousness that can save you.

This is the name which he will be called: **The Lord our Righteous Savior.** - Jeremiah 23:6

And know that, one day, your battle will be over. You will share in this victory.

The fruit of that righteousness will be peace; its effect will be quietness and confidence forever. - Isaiah 32:17

Protect your heart. Cover yourself with the breastplate.

Take a moment to read Matthew 6:33. What does this
verse say to you?

_____

_____

_____

_____

_____

_____

_____

_____

_____

_____

_____

_____

_____

_____

_____

_____

_____

_____

_____

_____

_____

_____

_____

_____

_____

_____

_____

_____

_____

_____

_____

PRAYER

Father,

I thank You for the constant protection You offer me. I am thankful that, despite the enemy's constant attacks, You cover me in Your armor and You defend me without fail. I am imperfect, Lord, and I will stumble at times in battle, but righteousness will always protect my heart. Never my own righteousness – I always fall short – but always Your righteousness, which never falters.

Righteousness is the only wealth in Your kingdom, Father, and the only thing that can produce peace. I thank you for this gift and I ask that you continue Your work in me until completion. Continue to cast out things that are not of You and replace them with things that are. Remake my thoughts and reshape my entire life, Lord, until it is good in Your eyes.

I thank You for Your righteousness, and for allowing me to always stay under the protection of it. Strengthen me to live every day in a way that shows my thankfulness to You, Father.

Amen.

DAY 9

GOSPEL OF PEACE

Dearest Son,

March on. March toward high places and along the perfect path I have laid out before you. Keep your eyes fixed on Me, and be aware that as you do the enemy lays traps at your feet seeking to ensnare you.

...and with your feet fitted with the readiness that comes from the gospel of peace. - Ephesians 6:15

In all things - marriage, family, parenting, religion, career, ministry, life - keep your feet fitted with the protection that only I can give; that is the gospel of peace.

I have told you these things, so that in me you may have peace. In this world you will have trouble. But take heart! I have overcome the world. - John 16:33

The life of Christ, his example, his love, his death and resurrection, this is the only thing that continuously wins out. The only gospel of truth and of peace. When your feet are fitted, and your every step protected with the gospel of Christ, the enemy's traps are wasted on you.

And the peace of God, which transcends all understanding, will guard your hearts and minds in Christ Jesus. - Philippians 4:7

March on, My son, with My truth guiding your steps, My righteousness guarding your heart, and My redemptive work wrapped all around you.

He provided redemption for His people; He ordained His covenant forever - holy and awesome is His name! - Psalm 111:9

All of these things, and your eyes fixed on Me.

Do you have peace? If not, what are the things that rob you of your peace on a persistent basis?

_____

_____

_____

_____

_____

_____

_____

_____

_____

_____

_____

_____

_____

_____

_____

_____

_____

_____

_____

_____

_____

_____

_____

_____

_____

_____

_____

_____

_____

_____

_____

_____

PRAYER

Father,

I ask, with everything I have, that You guide and protect my steps. I fit my feet with Your gospel of peace, Lord, and ask that you continuously show me my next step. Guide me down Your path.

Lead me to words and actions that empower my wife and strengthen our marriage. Provide me wisdom every day that allows me to raise children that fully understand what love is, and that look to You in all things. Help me understand what You desire of me day in and day out, Father. Show me how to spend my time, and warn me when to turn away. Help me to lead others to You, so that lives may be changed and souls might be saved.

I thank You, Father, for the victory You provide us. I thank You for the freedom of Your gospel. You have saved me, Lord, and I ask for the strength to march every day with the flag of Your redemption, Your covenant, Your salvation waving above me.

Amen.

DAY 10

SHIELD OF FAITH

Dearest Son,

The temptations of this world seek to inflame your mind and your heart.

With bitterness archers attacked him; they shot at him with hostility. - Genesis 49:23

These are the flaming arrows of the evil one - meaning not to set you on fire for God, but to set you on fire *against* God in favor of worldly things. These arrows come at you without ceasing and from all directions, and if an arrow finds its mark, it can cause extreme pain and sorrow.

In addition to all this, take up the shield of faith, with which you can extinguish all the flaming arrows of the evil one. - Ephesians 6:16

I call you to take up My shield, the shield of faith in God, to defend against these destructive things.

MY LOVE IS YOUR SHIELD.

Surely, Lord, you bless the righteous; you surround them with your favor as with a shield. - Psalm 5:12

MY WORD IS YOUR SHIELD.

Every word of God is flawless; he is a shield to those who take refuge in Him. - Proverbs 30:5

MY BLESSINGS ARE YOUR SHIELD.

For the Lord God is a sun and shield; the Lord bestows favor and honor; no good thing does he withhold from those whose walk is blameless. - Psalm 84:11

I AM YOUR SHIELD.

After this, the word of the Lord came to Abram in a vision: "Do not be afraid, Abram. I am your shield, your very great reward." - Genesis 15:1

When the enemy's arrow pierces you, it damages you in all aspects. Your heart, mind, soul, and spirit are inflamed with worldly things, your vision is compromised, and you begin living outside of My perfect plan for you. You are only partly alive.

Continue in battle, My son, wrapped in My armor and with Me standing before you as an impenetrable shield from the enemy. This is the shield of faith.

For no word from God will ever fail. - Luke 1:37

Describe a time in your life when you pursued
something or someone that turned out to be
destructive?

_____

_____

_____

_____

_____

_____

_____

_____

_____

_____

_____

_____

_____

_____

_____

_____

_____

_____

_____

_____

_____

_____

_____

_____

_____

_____

_____

_____

PRAYER

Father,

I know that I am always under fire. The enemy throws things at me constantly that are designed to break my concentration, to remove my eyes and my mind and my heart from You. If any of these arrows find their mark, it inflames my flesh and corrupts my spirit. It ruins my vision and weighs down my life. I don't want to be delayed or distracted or kept from any of the things You have for me, God. I want the abundant life You promise.

I am so thankful for the protection of Your shield, Father. So thankful that I can surround myself with Your love, and that I can take refuge in Your word. That You bestow so many blessings upon me – You are my sun and shield, Lord. As I go into battle each day – fighting for my heart and mind – I ask that You continue to walk before me as my protector, that You cover me as a shield against the evil one.

I cling to the shield of faith, Father, and lean on Your promises. For Your word will never fail.

Amen.

DAY 11

HELMET OF SALVATION

Dearest Son,

To battle the enemy with your head exposed is a great risk. He seeks to confuse your thoughts, to distract you, to weary you so that your head is lowered when he strikes.

Take the helmet of salvation… - Ephesians 6:17

Take on the emblem of Christ, and of the salvation only He can offer, and adorn your head with it. This is the symbol of your King, the crest of the kingdom to which you are an heir. I have claimed you and you fight in My name, just as I have battled against the darkness for your heart, mind, and soul.

He put on righteousness as his breastplate, and the helmet of salvation on his head; - Isaiah 59:17

Let the helmet of salvation continually purge old thoughts and renew them in My spirit.

Do not conform to the pattern of this world, but be transformed by the renewing of your mind. Then you will be able to test and approve what God's will is—his good, pleasing and perfect will. - Romans 12:2

Let the helmet of salvation continually deflect confusion - a primary weapon of the enemy - and replace it with peace and assuredness in My love for you.

But since we belong to the day, let us be sober, putting on faith and love as a breastplate, and the hope of salvation as a helmet. - 1 Thessalonians 5:8

Let the helmet of salvation strengthen you in battle and keep your head high even when you are weary. You don't fight in your own strength, but through Mine, and I will keep you upright.

The LORD is my strength and my defense; he has become my salvation. He is my God,
And I will praise him, my father's God, and I will exalt him. – Exodus 15:2

The term "thought battle" refers to the enemy planting thoughts in your mind that are designed to rob your peace and joy. Can you think of something you continually worry, obsess, or stress over?

_____
_____
_____
_____
_____
_____
_____
_____
_____
_____
_____
_____
_____
_____
_____
_____
_____
_____
_____
_____
_____
_____
_____
_____
_____
_____
_____
_____

PRAYER

Father,

My mind is a battlefield, and I look to you as my King. I ask You to lead me into battle and on to victory. The enemy seeks always to confuse my thoughts, to plant the lies of doubt and the seeds of sin in my mind. He looks to poison that which should remain pure for You. He wants me distracted. He wants my head down, so he can strike, instead of upward, looking toward You.

I claim the helmet of Your salvation as my protection, Lord. I take the cross of Christ and adorn my head with it. I ask that You end my old way of thinking and replace it with a renewing of my mind. Fill me with Your spirit, Father, so that I may hold every thought captive and test it against Your will for me. Remove confusion, remove doubt, remove fear, remove worry, and let me deflect every thought that is not of You. Strengthen me to think in the Spirit and not the flesh. To reflect my Father, and not the world.

I will cover myself with Your salvation, Lord. Give me the strength to continue this path of renewal You've set me on, and never let me forget Your faithfulness. I thank You for transformation, Lord. I thank You for new life.

Amen.

DAY 12

SWORD OF THE SPIRIT

Dearest Son,

You are prepared for battle. You stand ready to defend yourself.

Your waist is wrapped in the protection of My truth.
Your heart is covered with My righteousness.
Your steps are guided by My gospel of peace.
You are shielded by faith in Me, and the arrows of the enemy fail to penetrate.
Your head is covered by the helmet of salvation.

But what weapon are you wielding? How will you strike back? Yes, cover yourself against attack, but also march forward and cut him down - remove his influence from your life.

...and the sword of the Spirit, which is the word of God. - Ephesians 6:17

Resting in the belt of truth is the sword of the Spirit, My word, and it is time to pull it from its sheath and strike back at the enemy. You are not a victim, nor are you unarmed. I have handed this sword down to you, My son, and I ask you to use it.

My word will cut down the enemy.

For the word of God is living and active, sharper than any two-edged sword, piercing to the division of soul and of spirit, of joints and of marrow, and discerning the thoughts and intentions of the heart. - Hebrews 4:12

My word is life.

But he answered, "It is written, "'Man shall not live by bread alone, but by every word that comes from the mouth of God.'" - Matthew 4:4

My word has always been.

In the beginning was the Word, and the Word was with God, and the Word was God. - John 1:1

My word will always be.

But the word of the Lord remains forever. And this word is the good news that was preached to you. - 1 Peter 1:25

Your heart and mind and soul is of the utmost value to Me - defend them with every ounce of energy you have.

For you equipped me with strength for the battle; you made those who rise against me sink under me. - Psalm 18:39

Set aside time today to meet with God in His Word.
Read Luke 15:11-32 and describe what this passage says
to you.

_____
_____
_____
_____
_____
_____
_____
_____
_____
_____
_____
_____
_____
_____
_____
_____
_____
_____
_____
_____
_____
_____
_____
_____
_____
_____
_____
_____
_____
_____

PRAYER

Father,

Please strengthen me and equip me. I stand covered in your armor – fully protected by Your love, Your salvation, Your redemption. Now I ask that You build me up, that You arm me with the only weapon of any use in this battle, Lord. Arm me with Your word. I will not stand unarmed in this fight, Father, so I will come to Your word each day seeking wisdom, truth, guidance, instruction, comfort, peace, joy, promise, and protection. Above all, I come to Your word to seek You and to know You better.

When the enemy sends his lies, I will cut them down with Your word. When death is spoken over me, I will find life in Your word. I will continue to renew my mind and protect my heart with Your word. It has always been, and it will always be.

I will seek You every day, Father, and I thank You for Your faithfulness in always meeting me where I am. I will cover myself in Your armor, Lord, but I will also arm myself with Your word as I know that You always equip me with strength for the battle.

Amen.

DAY 13

FEAR

Dearest Son,

What is your greatest fear? What is it that scares you?

Lack of purpose?
Lack of money?
Rejection?
Transparency?
Honesty?
Abandonment?

All of your fears are wasted energy, and are arrows from the enemy that have taken root in your life. They muzzle you and hold you back from moving fully into the life I have created you to live. Your fears water down the freedom that I pour into you.

For the Spirit God gave us does not make us timid, but gives us power, love and self-discipline. - 2 Timothy 1:7

You should fear one thing and one thing only - separation from Me, your Father.

To fear Me is life.

The fear of the LORD leads to life; then one rests content, untouched by trouble. - Proverbs 19:23

To fear Me is wisdom.

The fear of the LORD is the beginning of wisdom; all who follow his precepts have good understanding. To him belongs eternal praise. - Psalm 111:10

To fear Me is to oppose the enemy.

To fear the LORD is to hate evil. - Proverbs 8:13

To fear Me is to save your own life.

The fear of the LORD is a fountain of life, turning a person from the snares of death. - Proverbs 14:27

My son - to fear Me is to **fear nothing else**.

The LORD is my shepherd, I lack nothing. He makes me lie down in green pastures, he leads me beside quiet waters, he refreshes my soul.
He guides me along the right paths for his name's sake. Even though I walk through the darkest valley, I will fear no evil, for you are with me; your rod and your staff, they comfort me.
You prepare a table before me in the presence of my enemies. You anoint my head with oil; my cup overflows. Surely your goodness and love will follow me all the days of my life and I will dwell in the house of the LORD forever. - Psalm 23:1-6

Write down your greatest fear, then attempt to
remember the first time you felt that fear. What was the
situation and who was involved? Repeat that process
for additional fears if necessary.

_____

_____

_____

_____

_____

_____

_____

_____

_____

_____

_____

_____

_____

_____

_____

_____

_____

_____

_____

_____

_____

_____

_____

_____

_____

_____

_____

_____

PRAYER

Father,

I take any and all fears I have about worldly things and I lay them at Your feet. You are the provider of all things, and Your child should never live in fear under Your provision. I won't let the effects of past hurts and mistakes cause me to live less than the abundant life You promise. I ask that You continue to cover me in freedom – pour it into me until it overflows and is apparent to others, Lord. Remove all fear from my heart and leave only the fear of you, God.

Let me always be reminded of Your constant presence, and let that knowledge bring me peace and contentment. Impart a heavenly wisdom into me, Father, and let me seek fountains of living waters in all I do. Let my fear of separation from You always turn me away from evil and death and toward love and life.

Let the fear of separation from you, Father, dictate my every decision and action. It is this fear that leads to power. And to peace and rest. When I fear You, I have no need to fear anything else.

Amen.

DAY 14

WHO IS LEADING?

Dearest Son,

If you aren't walking with Me so your children can see, then who are they watching?
If you aren't honoring and loving the woman I gave you, who is?
If you aren't battling for the spiritual peace of your house on a daily basis, then who will win it?

Son, who is leading?

Your family looks to you to live as an example of Christ, a light that points others toward Me.

You are the light of the world. A town built on a hill cannot be hidden. Neither do people light a lamp and put it under a bowl. Instead they put it on its stand, and it gives light to everyone in the house. In the same way, let your light shine before others, that they may see your good deeds and glorify your Father in heaven. - Matthew 5:14-16

Your daughters are learning how a man is to treat a woman, how a father is to treat his children. What have they learned from you today? What will they learn from you tomorrow?

A new command I give you: Love one another. As I have loved you, so you must love one another. By this everyone will know that you are my disciples, if you love one another. - John 13:34-35

Your son seeks to imitate you in all things. What is he imitating? What model are you giving him?

Whatever you have learned or received or heard from me, or seen in me—put it into practice. And the God of peace will be with you. - Philippians 4:9

Are you living out all of the blessings of marriage on a daily basis?

Husbands, love your wives, just as Christ loved the church and gave himself up for her to make her holy, cleansing her by the washing with water through the word, and to present her to himself as a radiant church, without stain or wrinkle or any other blemish, but holy and blameless. - Ephesians 5:25-27

I have opened My hand and blessed you with a family, and this is also a great responsibility. I ask you to battle on their behalf, son. Battle in prayer and in love and with words that water their spirit. Battle for their hearts.

Let us then approach God's throne of grace with confidence, so that we may receive mercy and find grace to help us in our time of need. - Hebrews 4:16

If you are married – ask God to reveal your wife's greatest need.
If you have children – ask God to reveal your children's greatest need.
Write them down, and commit to praying for these needs today.

_____

_____

_____

_____

_____

_____

_____

_____

_____

_____

_____

_____

_____

_____

_____

_____

_____

_____

_____

_____

_____

_____

_____

_____

_____

_____

_____

_____

PRAYER

Father,

I ask You to help me in being an example My children can look to in all things. Not an example based on my own abilities or strengths, but an example in complete and total reliance upon You, Lord.

Let them see me loving my wife the way she deserves to be loved. Let them see me comfort her and honor her and cover her in prayer. Let them see me pray peace over our house, casting all things out that are not of You.

Make me a light, Lord. A light that shines in the darkness and that always leads my family to You. If they misstep, or if they stumble, give me the wisdom and strength to help guide them back to Your light. Help me model a godly husband and father for my daughters. Strengthen me to be an example to my son. Make me a man.

The family You have blessed me with makes me rich beyond understanding. I ask that You make me a good steward of this wealth, God. Despite my weaknesses, my flaws, my mistakes, please continue to make me a better reflection of You, Father. Continue Your work in me. Equip me to lead those I love most.

Amen.

DAY 15

THE JOURNEY

Dearest Son,

What are you thinking about? What plans are you making?
Son, those things you plan and worry over and arrange and re-arrange that are days, weeks, months, even years away - what are you missing right now?

It is fine to think about the future, and to pray about what steps to take, but do not lean on your own wisdom and strength to see those plans through. Bring your future to Me in prayer.

Do not be anxious about anything, but in every situation, by prayer and petition, with thanksgiving, present your requests to God. - Philippians 4:6

Always trust that I am shaping your life according to My perfect plan for you.

Trust in the LORD with all your heart and lean not on your own understanding; in all your ways submit to him, and he will make your paths straight. - Proverbs 3:5-6

Be patient and wait for My timing.

The plans of the diligent lead to profit as surely as haste leads to poverty. - Proverbs 21:5

Continually seek My guidance along the way.

The wisdom of the prudent is to give thought to their ways, but the folly of fools is deception. - Proverbs 14:8

And son, most importantly, do not miss the journey that I am taking you on. Do not miss the opportunity to hug your daughters, to laugh with your son. Hold their hands. Kiss your wife. These blessings are too often overlooked by those looking too far ahead. Count my blessings in minutes, not in days. In steps, not in miles. To miss today's blessings because your eyes are fixed on the future can only lead to regret. You will truly know joy when you understand life in this way. You are closest to your Father when you embrace the journey we are taking together.

Every good and perfect gift is from above, coming down from the Father of the heavenly lights, who does not change like shifting shadows. - James 1:17

What things continually pull your thoughts into the future and away from the present moment? What might you be missing because of this?

_____

_____

_____

_____

_____

_____

_____

_____

_____

_____

_____

_____

_____

_____

_____

_____

_____

_____

_____

_____

_____

_____

_____

_____

_____

_____

_____

_____

_____

_____

PRAYER

Father,

For so long I have lived believing that I was in control of my own future, that failure or success rested on me. I thought and worried constantly about next steps, about tomorrow, next week, next year, and pored over my own plans. This was a mistake, Lord. This was an abundance of wasted time and energy. I ask that You forgive me, and that you help me to transform my thinking in this area.

I ask that You help me to replace the time I would have spent worrying and planning with time seeking You, God. Replace it with a mindset of living completely in each moment, not willing to miss even the smallest blessing of time with my family. When they ask for my time, help me to answer *yes* as often as I possibly can.

Help me to count steps, not miles. To live in every moment, as we get none of them back. Open my eyes to the journey, Lord. Show me what I am missing before it's gone.

Father, my prayer is to stand before You as a good steward of that most precious gift: TIME. I want the journey, God. I want the moments. I will seek these, and trust You in all the rest.

Amen.

DAY 16

RAVAGED BY WAR

Dearest Son,

The warfare is not hard to see. It is all around you. My children are ravaged by war.

The acts of the flesh are obvious: sexual immorality, impurity and debauchery; idolatry and witchcraft; hatred, discord, jealousy, fits of rage, selfish ambition, dissensions, factions and envy; drunkenness, orgies, and the like. I warn you, as I did before, that those who live like this will not inherit the kingdom of God. - Galatians 5:19-21

These are the crimes of the flesh - the fruit of those who exist without My spirit to guide them. These are battles that the enemy is winning against My sons and daughters. Their hearts and minds are being destroyed because they do not seek My protection. They do not cover with My armor.

Flesh: the physical nature of human beings

The flesh is completely at odds with Me and with the spiritual freedom only I can give you.

So I say, walk by the Spirit, and you will not gratify the desires of the flesh. - Galatians 5:16

You cannot please Me and please your flesh - you cannot do both.

Those who are in the realm of the flesh cannot please God. - Romans 8:8

The flesh is a moment of passing happiness, while My spirit is infinite joy and peace.

The mind governed by the flesh is death, but the mind governed by the Spirit is life and peace. - Romans 8:6

The flesh is the definition of weakness. Those who want power can find it only through Me.

For it is we who are the circumcision, we who serve God by his Spirit, who boast in Christ Jesus, and who put no confidence in the flesh - Philippians 3:3

Son, you must die to your flesh daily. The enemy wants at all times to steal back the territory you have claimed in My name. Your flesh will rage against you, but through Christ the flesh is crucified.

For we know that our old self was crucified with him so that the body ruled by sin might be done away with, that we should no longer be slaves to sin - Romans 6:6

In what areas do you continually give in to your flesh? How would your life be different if you gained victory in these areas?

_____

_____

_____

_____

_____

_____

_____

_____

_____

_____

_____

_____

_____

_____

_____

_____

_____

_____

_____

_____

_____

_____

_____

_____

_____

_____

_____

_____

PRAYER

Father,

I acknowledge that the war is all around, and it is neverending. The battle of the flesh against the spirit is constant, and so many of Your children are ravaged by it. Our flesh rises up against us in anger, hatred, greed, impatience, lust, and pride. These are of the enemy, Lord, and I ask that You strengthen me against these things.

Remind me, Father, that my flesh is a picture of pure weakness. That my reactions and responses to things are flawed – and weak – and that living in Your spirit is joy, peace, comfort, happiness, and purpose. Your spirit is power.

Continue to cover me in Your armor, God, and arm me with the Sword of the Spirit. Strengthen me for battle. Let me die to myself daily, and in so doing I come before You ready to pursue all that You have for me. The sacrifice of Your Son releases me from the bondage of sin, and I ask that You empower me to defend the territory of my heart and mind, every day, and that I not relinquish anything back to the enemy. Apart from You I am ravaged by this war. With You I will continue to claim victory, Father.

Amen.

DAY 17

CHASING SHADOWS

Dearest Son,

What you see in the world is one mirage after another. What from a distance looks worthy, is just an empty shadow up close. Yet, my children chase these things. Day after day, My sons and daughters chase these shadows and day after day they remain unfulfilled. Unhappy, and without purpose.

What the world sees as power has no power in it.

But you are not to be like that. Instead, the greatest among you should be like the youngest, and the one who rules like the one who serves. - Luke 22:26

Son, chase true power.

I have given you authority to trample on snakes and scorpions and to overcome all the power of the enemy; nothing will harm you. - Luke 10:19

What the world sees as happiness is filled only with sorrow.

When you sit to dine with a ruler, note well what is before you, and put a knife to your throat if you are given to gluttony. Do not crave his delicacies, for that food is deceptive. - Proverbs 23:1-3

Son, chase true happiness.

Rejoice in the Lord always. I will say it again: Rejoice! - Philippians 4:4

What the world sees as wealth is the truest poverty.

Now listen, you rich people, weep and wail because of the misery that is coming on you. Your wealth has rotted, and moths have eaten your clothes. Your gold and silver are corroded. Their corrosion will testify against you and eat your flesh like fire. - James 1:1-3

Son, chase true wealth.

The blessing of the LORD brings wealth, without painful toil for it. - Proverbs 10:22

So many of My children waste their entire lives chasing shadows. Live with purpose, and chase what matters. Chase Me.

Seek the LORD while he may be found; call on him while he is near. Let the wicked forsake their ways and the unrighteous their thoughts. Let them turn to the LORD, and he will have mercy on them, and to our God, for he will freely pardon. - Isaiah 55: 6-7

What, do you believe, would bring you happiness?

_____
_____
_____
_____
_____
_____
_____
_____
_____
_____
_____
_____
_____
_____
_____
_____
_____
_____
_____
_____
_____
_____
_____
_____
_____
_____
_____
_____
_____

PRAYER

Father,

I ask that Your Spirit offer me a constant reminder about what has significance and what does not. Show me what matters, and what does not. Give me the wisdom to pursue things of eternal consequence, and also the wisdom to avoid things that do not. Lead me away from the shadows and distractions of the enemy, and toward the work You lay out before me.

Lord, keep me away from all things that cause weakness. I seek the only real power – the power that is found in serving You.

Keep me from all sources of sorrow and despair. I seek real happiness, so I will rejoice in You and all You are.

Keep me from poverty and misery, God. Let me always understand the true meaning of wealth, and always praise You as the source of blessing.

I want to make the most of the time You have given me here, Father. I want to spend my minutes seeking You, chasing You, calling out to You and pursuing what You have laid out for me. Keep me out of the shadows and let me always stand in Your light. Amen.

DAY 18

THANKFUL

Dearest Son,

I want you to take this entire day to be thankful. You have battled. You have fought hard. The war is not over, but in the midst of the fighting I ask you to stop down and spend time being thankful.

Sing and make music from your heart to the Lord, always giving thanks to God the Father for everything, in the name of our Lord Jesus Christ. – Ephesians 5:19-20

It won't take much to see what to be thankful for (look around you), but it is important that you remember the object of your thankfulness. Be thankful to Me, your good and faithful Father.

Be thankful for who I am.

Give thanks to the Lord, for he is good; his love endures forever. – Psalm 107:1

Be thankful at all times. Even in the midst of trials, I still hold you in my arms. I am teaching and growing you in these times.

Give thanks in all circumstances; for this is God's will for you in Christ Jesus. – 1 Thessalonians 5:18

Never cease to be thankful.

That my heart may sing your praises and not be silent. Lord my God, I will praise you forever. – Psalm 30:12

Be thankful to Me for the gift of Jesus Christ.

Thanks be to God for his indescribable gift! – 2nd Corinthians 9:15

That is, the gift of your freedom.

But thanks be to God! He gives us the victory through our Lord Jesus Christ. – 1 Corinthians 15:57

Write down everything you are thankful for.

_____
_____
_____
_____
_____
_____
_____
_____
_____
_____
_____
_____
_____
_____
_____
_____
_____
_____
_____
_____
_____
_____
_____
_____
_____
_____
_____
_____
_____
_____

PRAYER

Father,

Today, I am thankful. I am thankful that You opened my eyes to another day. I am thankful for the beauty of Your creation as the sun rises in the east and paints Your majesty across the morning sky. I am thankful to kiss the foreheads of my children every morning, for being able to hold and pray protection over my wife, and for the ability to tell them all that I love them. And I am thankful that they love me back.

I am thankful for Your constant reminders and the wisdom You provide. The wisdom to never wish my days away, but instead to slow time down and to exist – to be completely present – in every moment. I am thankful that, even when times are difficult and my spirit seems tired, that You raise me up and You always teach me something new about Your ways. I am thankful that You are faithful to meet me everywhere I am, whether strong and upright or broken down – You meet me there.

I am thankful for who You are, Lord. I am thankful that You love me, that You battled to win back my heart and mind and soul, and that I've been bought with a price. I am thankful for the cross. And for the blessed hope of Your eternal kingdom. I am thankful for the fact that You use imperfect vessels like me to accomplish Your perfect will, and for the fact that You might still have work for me to do during my time here. I am thankful for purpose. Thankful for possibilities beyond my comprehension. For accomplishments beyond my abilities. And I am Thankful for Your path and for the light You shine to keep me on it.

I am thankful for forgiveness. Thankful for never-ending love. Thankful for victory. And thankful for freedom.

Amen.

DAY 19

MY TREASURE

Treasure: something valuable that is hidden or kept in a safe place
Treasure: something that is very special, important, or valuable

Dearest Son,

I treasure your heart. It is of enormous value to Me. Your entire life is an overflow from your heart. However, when not filled with My spirit, the heart is toxic, sick, and filled with despair.

Don't you see that whatever enters the mouth goes into the stomach and then out of the body? But the things that come out of a person's mouth come from the heart, and these defile them. For out of the heart come evil thoughts—murder, adultery, sexual immorality, theft, false testimony, slander. - Matthew 15:17-19

Apart from Me, the heart cannot be trusted nor understood.

The heart is deceitful above all things and beyond cure. Who can understand it? - Jeremiah 17:9

Many believe that the heart is irreparable, that it cannot ever be healed. But I am constantly seeking your heart, weighing your heart. I desperately want this treasure for My own.

But the LORD said to Samuel, "Do not consider his appearance or his height, for I have rejected him. The LORD does not look at the things people look at. People look at the outward appearance, but the LORD looks at the heart." - 1 Samuel 16:7

Your greatest challenge on a daily basis is to protect this treasure, to protect and guard your heart from all of the attacks of the enemy.

Above all else, guard your heart, for everything you do flows from it. - Proverbs 4:23

Come to Me continually for the mending and renewal of your heart.

I will give them an undivided heart and put a new spirit in them; I will remove from them their heart of stone and give them a heart of flesh. - Ezekiel 11:19

Approach Me always with true belief in your heart.

For it is with your heart that you believe and are justified, and it is with your mouth that you profess your faith and are saved. - Romans 10:10

Wash your heart clean and pure through Christ alone.

May he strengthen your hearts so that you will be blameless and holy in the presence of our God and Father when our Lord Jesus comes with all his holy ones. - 1 Thessalonians 3:13

My son, guard this treasure with all you have. Do not allow even a small piece of it to be given outside of My will for you. Call out to Me, your Father, for constant renewal and strength.

Create in me a pure heart, O God, and renew a steadfast spirit within me. - Psalm 51:10

What do you believe about your own heart?

_____
_____
_____
_____
_____
_____
_____
_____
_____
_____
_____
_____
_____
_____
_____
_____
_____
_____
_____
_____
_____
_____
_____
_____
_____
_____

PRAYER

Father,

I ask that You forgive me for all of the times I have been reckless with my heart. For all of the times I did not love and protect my heart, and did not value this treasure in the same way You do. I understand now how relentlessly You seek after my heart, how much You want it for Your own, and I desire to treat it and protect it in a way that pleases You.

So many times, the overflow of my heart has brought pain and darkness into my life. I allowed in poisonous things, the arrows of the enemy, and these spilled over into my walk with You and with those You've given me. I lift all of this up to You and ask for restoration.

I ask for Your help in protecting my heart, Lord. Strengthen me to guard it from all things that are not of You. Empower me to protect it from all distraction, all wasted effort, and all things that are outside of Your will for my life. If I look to something other than You for peace, happiness, or purpose,

I ask that Your Spirit shine a light that directs me back to Your path. Retrieve for me the pieces of my heart that have been carelessly cast away, and create in me a whole and mended heart. Renew my heart, repair it, strengthen it, and allow me to come to You with a heart of faith, God. I ask for the full renewal of my heart that can only be found in Jesus Christ. Make me clean and pure before You, so that others may see the work of Your hands and desire it for themselves. I lift this treasure up to You and ask that You take full possession of it. Make it new again and create a steadfast spirit within me, Father.

I ask that You renew me every day, Lord. Restore me stronger than before. And give me the strength and wisdom to protect and defend what You value so highly.

Amen.

DAY 20

BURIED ALIVE

Dearest Son,

What do you see now that your eyes are opened? Look around and tell me what you see. The hearts of my children are beating, their lungs are breathing, but they are not living. This is only half of an existence. Half of what I created them to be.

They are buried alive.

As for you, you were dead in your transgressions and sins, in which you used to live when you followed the ways of this world and of the ruler of the kingdom of the air, the spirit who is now at work in those who are disobedient. - Ephesians 2:1-3

They have allowed the enemy to continue to pile guilt, regret, worry, and bondage on them to the point that they can barely move. They are trapped beneath the garbage.

The god of this age has blinded the minds of unbelievers, so that they cannot see the light of the gospel that displays the glory of Christ, who is the image of God. - 2 Corinthians 4:4

My children must understand that I created them for so much more.

83

Yet for us there is but one God, the Father, from whom all things came and for whom we live; and there is but one Lord, Jesus Christ, through whom all things came and through whom we live.
- 1 Corinthians 8:6

Rise up! On My power, dig out of the pit you've been buried in.

He gives strength to the weary and increases the power of the weak. - Isaiah 40:29

My children do not lay as corpses - they walk in power as sons and daughters of the Lord Your God, and as heirs of My kingdom.

And when the Chief Shepherd appears, you will receive the crown of glory that will never fade away. - 1 Peter 5:4

In My power comes freedom, comes purpose, comes strength, comes full and abundant life. This is the desire of the Father for His children.

This is what the LORD says—your Redeemer, who formed you in the womb:
I am the LORD, the Maker of all things, who stretches out the heavens, who spreads out the earth by myself - Isaiah 44:24

Have life!

Then Jesus declared, "I am the bread of life. Whoever comes to me will never go hungry, and whoever believes in me will never be thirsty. - John 6:3

What "garbage" would you eliminate from your life if
you felt you could?

_____

_____

_____

_____

_____

_____

_____

_____

_____

_____

_____

_____

_____

_____

_____

_____

_____

_____

_____

_____

_____

_____

_____

_____

_____

_____

_____

_____

_____

PRAYER

Father,

I thank You for what it means to belong to You. For what it means to live – to live fully and abundantly – and to always be moving toward being what You created me to be. I was dead in sin, Lord, and you removed that from me. You washed away the guilt, the regret, the bondage, and raised me up to walk in victory and to live with power.

Thank You for opening my eyes, Father. Thank you for standing me straight, for removing the weight that I carried for so long, and for washing me clean. I move now, God, into Your purpose for me. I move into the abundant life You promised, and I will wake up each day requesting strength from You. Requesting power from You. Asking that You make me a light for my family, and an encouragement to those who are in the same bondage that I once lived in – to show that just existing is not enough. A child of God has inherited full and abundant life.

I am no longer buried under the weight of sin, and I thank You. Fill me with Your Spirit so that, as You promise, I will never go hungry. I will never be thirsty. Push me forward to take on all that You have promised for me in this life, Father. Make full use of me until my time here is complete. Amen.

DAY 21

THE WAY

Dearest Son,

Hear this clearly:

I am **the way** *and the truth and the life.* - John 14:6

I am the only way to all of the things you were designed for.

I am the way to forgiveness.

If we confess our sins, he is faithful and just and will forgive us our sins and purify us from all unrighteousness. - 1 John 1:9

I am the way to redemption.

For he has rescued us from the dominion of darkness and brought us into the kingdom of the Son he loves, in whom we have redemption, the forgiveness of sins. - Colossians 1:14

I am the way to restoration.

"Come to me, all you who are weary and burdened, and I will give you rest." - Matthew 11:28

I am the way to salvation.

For God so loved the world that he gave his one and only Son, that whoever believes in him shall not perish but have eternal life. - John 3:16

I am the way to wisdom.

If any of you lacks wisdom, you should ask God, who gives generously to all without finding fault, and it will be given to you. - James 1:5

I am the way to love.

Whoever does not love does not know God, because God is love. - 1 John 4:8

I am the way to freedom.

It is for freedom that Christ has set us free. Stand firm, then, and do not let yourselves be burdened again by a yoke of slavery. - Galatians 5:1

I am the way to the kingdom.

But in keeping with his promise we are looking forward to a new heaven and a new earth, where righteousness dwells. - 2 Peter 3:13

It is time that you rid yourself of all other methods, all other ways to finding the things that make you whole. They do nothing but cause you heartache and sickness. I am your Father, and I am the only way.

In your own words, define the term "restoration."

_____

_____

_____

_____

_____

_____

_____

_____

_____

_____

_____

_____

_____

_____

_____

_____

_____

_____

_____

_____

_____

_____

_____

_____

_____

_____

_____

_____

_____

PRAYER

Father,

I come to You thankful for offering me a way. For loving me enough to offer me a way – the only way – to enter into all of the incredible things I was designed for. I ask that You forgive me for any time in my life when I sought out other ways, was distracted by other things, and lost focus on my relationship with You.

You not only offer forgiveness, but You purify me and wash me clean. You not only rescue me from the darkness, but you fully redeem me and bring me into Your light. You not only allow me to bring You my burdens, but you remove them, offer me rest, and restore me completely. You love me so much that You offered your Son as a sacrifice for my weakness and my failures, and with that gift You give me eternal life. The kingdom of heaven is Yours, and only through You can we reach it.

Outside of You there is only sickness, pain, frustration, and defeat. You are the only way, and I will continue to seek You.

Amen.

DAY 22

THE TRUTH

Dearest Son,

I am the way and **the truth** *and the life.* - John 14:6

Son, truth does not exist apart from Me. I am the only truth, the author and creator of all things true. All other things are false - lies intended to separate you from your Father.

The truth is freedom.

Then you will know the truth, and the truth will set you free. - John 8:32

My word is the essence of truth.

All your words are true; all your righteous laws are eternal. - Psalm 119:160

Worship Me in truth.

God is spirit, and his worshipers must worship in the Spirit and in truth. - John 4:24

Call to Me in truth.

The LORD is near to all who call on him, to all who call on him in truth. - Psalm 145:18

The truth has been sent to guide you, counsel you, teach you, and comfort you.

But when he, the Spirit of truth, comes, he will guide you into all the truth. - John 16:13

My son, wrap yourself in My truth and test everything against it. Anything that is not of Me and that does not produce the fruit of the spirit cannot be truth, and therefore it must be a lie. These things are false and designed by the enemy to pull you away from your Father. Grab onto truth; blanket yourself in it, protect yourself with it, always seek it out. Wherever you find truth, you find Me also.

Read John 8:32.
What does this verse say to you?

_____

_____

_____

_____

_____

_____

_____

_____

_____

_____

_____

_____

_____

_____

_____

_____

_____

_____

_____

_____

_____

_____

_____

_____

_____

_____

_____

PRAYER

Father,

I lift all things up to You and ask that You lead me always to the truth. I know that You are the author and provider of all things that are true – You are the essence of truth. I ask that You equip me with the wisdom to recognize when the truth has been replaced with a lie. I ask that Your Spirit continue to guide me and teach me and turn me away from the lies of the enemy.

I ask for continued freedom in the truth, Lord. Allow me to know more about You and Your ways, as this is the only freedom that exists. I ask that You continue to imprint Your words onto my heart, and fix them in my mind, so that when I am presented with a lie I have the weapon to defend my freedom.

Hear me and meet me when I call to You, Lord. Allow me to worship You in truth and in spirit, and please meet me where I am. Strengthen me for battle. I will call to You, God, and ask that You equip me to defend the territories of my heart and mind – these that have been won in Your name.

I will test all things against Your truth. I will measure all things against the fruit of the spirit. Empower me to cast out lies, and to blanket myself in Your truth, Father. Wrap me in truth and let me live in it always. Amen.

DAY 23

AND THE LIFE

Dearest Son,

*I am the way and the truth and **the life**.* - John 14:6

Son, life does not exist apart from Me. If you follow My way and walk in My truth, you will find the life I have for you. Your Father is the source of all of these good things.

I am the author of life, speaking life into existence and breathing life into the first man.

Then the LORD God formed a man from the dust of the ground and breathed into his nostrils the breath of life, and the man became a living being. - Genesis 2:7

I am the definition of life. All things apart from Me are death.

His divine power has given us everything we need for a godly life through our knowledge of him who called us by his own glory and goodness. - 2 Peter 1:3

I have come to redeem life, to restore life to My children.

95

Then Jesus declared, "I am the bread of life. Whoever comes to me will never go hungry, and whoever believes in me will never be thirsty. - John 6:35

Life with your Father is more than you could ever imagine.

The thief comes only to steal and kill and destroy; I have come that they may have life, and have it to the full. - John 10:10

Son, hear this clearly:

Jesus answered, "I am the way and the truth and the life. No one comes to the Father except through me. - John 14:6

Do you believe you are experiencing everything God has for your life?

_____
_____
_____
_____
_____
_____
_____
_____
_____
_____
_____
_____
_____
_____
_____
_____
_____
_____
_____
_____
_____
_____
_____
_____
_____
_____
_____
_____

PRAYER

Father,

I lift myself up to You and acknowledge that You are the author of all life. You gave life to the first man and to all of mankind – without You and apart from You there is only death. You are not only the author of life, Lord, but You alone can sustain life and provide us the power to live with freedom, joy, and purpose as You have created us.

I thank you for the redemption of life that You offer. You take what was once dead and allow it to breath in life again. You provide new life to those walking in bondage and sin. You restore me and make me whole, and You allow me to approach Your throne for my every need and weakness.

I ask for the life of fullness and abundance that only You can offer. The enemy exists only to bring destruction and death – strengthen me against him and fill me with the life that comes from Your Spirit.

Father, You are the only way, the only truth, and the only life. Nothing exists outside of you except pain and fear. Please strengthen me to look to You in all things, at all times, and in every circumstance. You are my Father and my King. Amen.

DAY 24

PURPOSE

Dearest Son,

Are you living in fullness? Are you experiencing everything I have set aside for you? Or do you carry the weight of things I paid the price for long ago?

For God so loved the world that he gave his one and only Son, that whoever believes in him shall not perish but have eternal life.
- John 3:16

You have been washed clean and our relationship restored completely. My children cannot be separated from Me by anyone, anything, or for any reason.

For I am convinced that neither death nor life, neither angels nor demons, neither the present nor the future, nor any powers, neither height nor depth, nor anything else in all creation, will be able to separate us from the love of God that is in Christ Jesus our Lord.
- Romans 8:38

With this, you are made new. You are reborn.

Therefore, if anyone is in Christ, the new creation has come: the old is gone, the new is here! - 2 Corinthians 5:17

I have broken the chains that keep you from walking in fullness.

Therefore, there is now no condemnation for those who are in Christ Jesus, because through Christ Jesus the law of the Spirit who gives life has set you free from the law of sin and death. - Romans 8:1-2

What sets your heart on fire? What boils the passion within you? What is your purpose in this life? I speak into existence the things that seem impossible to you. I create your purpose, design your heart, and lay the path before you. I give you these things.

He draws up the drops of water, which distill down to the streams; the clouds pour down their moisture and abundant showers fall on mankind. - Job 36:27-28

You were created for far more than you can comprehend. You were designed to receive the abundance of what I have set aside for you, but before now you were not free to claim it. Claim it now.

Now to him who is able to do immeasurably more than all we ask or imagine, according to his power that is at work within us, to him be the glory in the church and in Christ Jesus throughout all generations, for ever and ever! - Ephesians 3:20

You cannot fathom the greatness of things to come. Walk with Me, seek Me, and see what I have for you.

However, as it is written:

"What no eye has seen, what no ear has heard, and what no human mind has conceived - the things God has prepared for those who love him - 1 Corinthians 2:9

If you could spend your days doing anything, with no concern over finances, what would you do?

_____

_____

_____

_____

_____

_____

_____

_____

_____

_____

_____

_____

_____

_____

_____

_____

_____

_____

_____

_____

_____

_____

_____

_____

_____

PRAYER

Father,

I thank You for the restoration of our relationship, and for Your Son who offers eternal life through His sacrifice. I thank You for new birth, for creating new life within me where there was only death, for washing me clean and making me whole again.

I ask now, Lord, that you break all chains that hold me back from walking in the fullness that You offer. My prayer is to keep my heart and mind on You at all times, and to seek out everything You have planned for me in this life. Set a fire within me, Lord. Let purpose boil inside of me, push me forward, and guide me along Your path.

Father, open my eyes to see my purpose and open my ears to hear You guide me to it. Let Your abundant showers fall down upon me, and let me follow You to the amazing things set aside for Your children. I ask for greatness, Lord. Not for my own sake, but so that You might be glorified. I ask for purpose, so that other lives might be touched.

I will continue to seek You in all that I do, Lord. I will walk with You in the hope that You will find me fit to be sent out. That you will find me worthy of the purpose You created and designed me for. I lay my life at Your feet and pray that You find me useful, God. I want to see all of what You have for me. I want to make a difference.

Amen.

DAY 25

NO MORE RUNNING

Dearest Son,

In the past, you have run from Me because you fear closeness. You turn away from Me because you fear anyone knowing you too well. But you must understand that your Father knows everything there is to know about you.

You know when I sit and when I rise; you perceive my thoughts from afar. You discern my going out and my lying down; you are familiar with all my ways. Before a word is on my tongue you, LORD, know it completely. - Psalm 139:2-4

Even the smallest detail about My children is known to Me.

And even the very hairs of your head are all numbered. - Matthew 10:30

Why do you run from this intimacy? Because you think I look to punish you.

For all have sinned and fall short of the glory of God. - Romans 3:23

You run from Me, looking for a place to hide, but you cannot.

Nothing in all creation is hidden from God's sight. Everything is uncovered and laid bare before the eyes of him to whom we must give account. - Hebrews 4:13

My son, you must know that I do not seek closeness in order to punish you. I seek closeness because you are My child and I love you.

For he chose us in him before the creation of the world to be holy and blameless in his sight. In love, he predestined us for adoption to sonship through Jesus Christ, in accordance with his pleasure and will— to the praise of his glorious grace, which he has freely given us in the One he loves. - Ephesians 1:4-6

No more running, son. No more hiding. From here on, I ask you to walk alongside your Father.

Walk in obedience to all that the LORD your God has commanded you, so that you may live and prosper and prolong your days in the land that you will possess. - Deuteronomy 5:33

Do you feel that your view of God has been skewed in
the past? In what way(s)?

_____
_____
_____
_____
_____
_____
_____
_____
_____
_____
_____
_____
_____
_____
_____
_____
_____
_____
_____
_____
_____
_____
_____
_____
_____
_____
_____
_____
_____

PRAYER

Father,

I am done running from You. I am finished running from closeness with You, with pretending I can find a place where You can't find me. Where you can't see my failures. You know all there is to know about me, and I choose now to rejoice in this. I choose to rejoice in the fact that You know all there is to know about me – all of my weaknesses and my faults and my shortcomings – and still You love me as a Father loves His son.

I am choosing now to run to You, Father. To seek You, call out to You, search for You, and run to You at all times and in all things. To seek Your face and reach for Your hand under all circumstances, God. I want to walk alongside You in every available moment. My thoughts, my actions, and every word I speak will be laid at Your feet. Guide me, mold me, and make a new heart in me, Lord.

My days of running from You are over. I will spend the rest of my days chasing after You, God. I only ask that You never stop allowing me to find You.

Amen.

DAY 26

PRIDE AND POWER

Dearest Son,

You have long confused pride with power, and pride with strength. You have long believed that you know what a man is, and how a man should act, but this is a mistake. You have taken hold of pride, which is a foothold for the enemy, and in doing so you have gained weakness.

Pride is an early symptom of a sick heart, and a sure sign of coming disgrace.

When pride comes, then comes disgrace, but with humility comes wisdom. - Proverbs 11:2

I love my children, therefore a prideful man is guaranteed to receive correction from Me.

The LORD detests all the proud of heart. Be sure of this: They will not go unpunished. - Proverbs 16:5

Your pride fools you into thinking you stand in high places, but the opposite is true.

Pride brings a person low, but the lowly in spirit gain honor. - Proverbs 29:23

With pride, the enemy has tricked you into believing that you walk as a conqueror. Son, you have been fooled.

The pride of your heart has deceived you, you who live in the clefts of the rocks and make your home on the heights, you who say to yourself, 'Who can bring me down to the ground?' - Obadiah 1:3

Pride is the sin of a weak man - one who has fallen captive to the enemy. Lay your pride down, son, and take up real power.

So that your faith might not rest on human wisdom, but on God's power. - 1 Corinthians 2:5

And real strength.

I can do all this through him who gives me strength. - Phillipians 4:13

True freedom.

But now that you have been set free from sin and have become slaves of God, the benefit you reap leads to holiness, and the result is eternal life. - Romans 6:22

And true purpose.

"I am the vine; you are the branches. If you remain in me and I in you, you will bear much fruit; apart from me you can do nothing. - John 15:5

Seek me, your Father, and you will break the chains of pride and understand what strength really is.

Do you feel that you have held to incorrect views of pride and power? How so?

_____

_____

_____

_____

_____

_____

_____

_____

_____

_____

_____

_____

_____

_____

_____

_____

_____

_____

_____

_____

_____

_____

_____

_____

_____

_____

_____

PRAYER

Father,

I ask that You forgive me for the years of accumulated pride in my life. Forgive me for thinking I knew what I should be, how I should act, and for being so confused about what You expect of me. I walked in pride and put myself on the throne of my own life. My pride allowed the enemy to take hold of my heart and harden it, poison it, and lead me into frustration and despair.

I lay my pride at Your feet, Lord, and ask You to cast it away. In its place, please fill me with Your Spirit. Allow me to lean on You alone for my strength. Let me not be fooled, God, and instead let Your heavenly wisdom fall upon me. I ask for Your strength where alone I would have weakness, and for Your freedom where alone I would fall prey to sin and bondage. Let me become captive to You.

Allow me to abide in You, Father, so that You can show me what strength truly is. Remove my pride, which does nothing but cause me to stumble and fall. Instead, show me my purpose and equip me to chase after it in Your name, Lord.

Amen.

DAY 27

THE TEST

Dearest Son,

Test all things - thoughts, actions, reactions - <u>all things</u> against the fruit of the spirit. This test will never fail you, and will never prove false. Measure everything that enters your mind against these things and you will know, without any doubt, if your thoughts and actions are of Me or if they are a ploy of the enemy.

Do the things in your life allow you to feel, or do, or be these things?

Love: unselfish loyal and benevolent concern for the good of another; warm attachment, enthusiasm, or devotion

Whoever does not love does not know God, because God is love. - 1 John 4:8

Joy: a state of happiness or felicity

A cheerful heart is good medicine, but a crushed spirit dries up the bones. - Proverbs 17:22

Peace: freedom from disquieting or oppressive thoughts or emotions

You will keep in perfect peace those whose minds are steadfast, because they trust in you. - Isaiah 26:3

Forbearance: the quality of someone who is patient and able to deal with a difficult person or situation without becoming angry

Whoever believes in the Son has eternal life, but whoever rejects the Son will not see life, for God's wrath remains on them. - John 3:36

Kindness: wanting and liking to do good things and to bring happiness to others

Be kind and compassionate to one another, forgiving each other, just as in Christ God forgave you. - Ephesians 4:32

Goodness: of a favorable character or tendency

How abundant are the good things that you have stored up for those who fear you, that you bestow in the sight of all, on those who take refuge in you. - Psalm 31:19

Faithfulness: having or showing true and constant support or loyalty

If we confess our sins, he is faithful and just and will forgive us our sins and purify us from all unrighteousness. - 1 John 1:9

Gentleness: having or showing a kind and quiet nature : not harsh or violent

To slander no one, to be peaceable and considerate, and always to be gentle toward everyone. - Titus 3:2

Self-Control: restraint exercised over one's own impulses, emotions, or desires

Like a city whose walls are broken through is a person who lacks self-control. - Proverbs 25:28

If there is anything in your life that does not produce these fruits, it has failed the test. If it does not lead you to the fruits of the spirit, which are blessings from your Father, then it is of the enemy and you must cast it away.

Measure your entire life in this way, son, and cast out those unfruitful things that drain life from you.

The fruits of the Holy Spirit are love, joy, peace, forbearance, kindness, goodness, faithfulness, gentleness, and self-control.
Take a moment to evaluate everything in your life, and write down the things that do not create these fruits.

PRAYER

Father,

I thank You for the ability to measure all things in my life against Your holiness. For the ability to test all thoughts, action, reactions, and motives against Your perfect strength and mercy. I ask that You would give me enough wisdom to recognize things or people in my life that do not offer the fruit of the spirit, and also for the strength and courage to change my life according to what You want for me. I ask for less of me and more of You, God.

Empower me to love in the same way that You love me. Allow me to seek out and find the joy that can only come from a closeness with You. Let me find peace in knowing that You are on the throne of my life, and that it is Your light that guides my steps. Strengthen me to act with forbearance and kindness to everyone who crosses my path, Lord, for this is the only way to show the work you've done in me.

Let me treat those I love most with kindness, goodness, faithfulness, gentleness, and self-control at all times, God. Please continue to work through my weaknesses and shortcomings to allow some small portion of Your greatness to shine through me so that others may see it.

I will continue to test all things in my life against Your Spirit, Father. Give me the wisdom and strength to remove anything that is not of You. Amen.

DAY 28

KNOW YOUR OWN STRENGTH

Dearest Son,

I ask you to understand your own strength. I want you to know what you're capable of, and to pursue life in this knowledge.

To understand strength, you must first understand weakness. Weakness is your unfortunate inheritance. Not earned by you, but yours nonetheless.

And the LORD God said, "The man has now become like one of us, knowing good and evil. He must not be allowed to reach out his hand and take also from the tree of life and eat, and live forever." - Genesis 3:22

You must understand the weakness of your position.

Then, after desire has conceived, it gives birth to sin; and sin, when it is full-grown, gives birth to death. - James 1:15

But know that you are not alone.

No temptation has overtaken you except what is common to mankind. - 1 Corinthians 10:13

Understanding weakness, you now can understand strength. I, your Father, am your strength.

I strengthen you.

I can do all this through him who gives me strength. -
Philippians 4:13

I help you, and I hold you up.

*So do not fear, for I am with you; do not be dismayed, for I am
your God. I will strengthen you and help you; I will uphold you
with my righteous right hand.* - Isaiah 41:10

I go with you into battle and deliver you to victory.

*For the LORD your God is the one who goes with you to fight for
you against your enemies to give you victory.* - Deuteronomy
20:4

I give you rest.

*"Come to me, all you who are weary and burdened, and I will
give you rest."* - Matthew 11:28

And I renew your strength.

But those who hope in the LORD will renew their strength. -
Isaiah 40:31

Son, you can accomplish nothing through your own
strength. But through the strength of your Father you
will take hold of life in ways that you never thought

possible. Know My strength, and you will know your own.

List situations in your life where you have relied on your own strength. Invite God into those situations today.

_____
_____
_____
_____
_____
_____
_____
_____
_____
_____
_____
_____
_____
_____
_____
_____
_____
_____
_____
_____
_____
_____
_____
_____
_____
_____
_____
_____
_____

PRAYER

Father,

I come to Your throne acknowledging my own weakness, acknowledging that the only true strength comes from You. I know that, without You, nothing can be accomplished in this life. But with You, nothing is impossible.

I ask you to strengthen me daily. Each morning when I wake up, I ask for Your spirit to fill me, Lord, and for You to empower me to battle for my own heart and mind day in and day out. Hold me up with Your right hand. Guide me into battle against the enemy and equip me to claim victory against his lies. Help me to test all things against Your word, and to fight against all things that are not of You and that do not represent the love and protection You offer me.

Give me rest and renewal, God. Allow me to come to You when I am weary, knowing that You are faithful to lift me back up, stand me up straight, and keep me on Your path. Remind me at all times, Father, that to rely on my own strength is to fall to pride. I will rely on Your strength through me, Lord, and I will continually seek You in all that I do.

Amen.

DAY 29

LOVE HAS WON

Dearest Son,

Love has won. In the battle for you, My son, and for your heart and soul - love has won.

For it is by grace you have been saved, through faith—and this is not from yourselves, it is the gift of God—not by works, so that no one can boast. - Ephesians 2:8-9

You have walked in bondage, separated from your Father for all this time.

As it is written:
There is no one righteous, not even one; there is no one who understands; there is no one who seeks God. All have turned away, they have together become worthless; there is no one who does good, not even one. - Romans 3:10-12

And now you turn back to Me, seeking Me, and you have found Me.

But if from there you seek the LORD your God, you will find him if you seek him with all your heart and with all your soul. - Deuteronomy 4:29

Call on the name of Jesus Christ, accept His saving work of redemption, and be separated from your Father no more.

For the wages of sin is death, but the gift of God is eternal life in Christ Jesus our Lord. - Romans 6:23

Your old self is no more - your thoughts, habits, actions, tendencies, attitudes, worries - they are no more. You are reborn; you are new.

Therefore, if anyone is in Christ, the new creation has come: The old has gone, the new is here! - 2 Corinthians 5:17

And I am the source of your strength, the source of all good things.

The LORD is my strength and my defense; he has become my salvation. He is my God, and I will praise him, my father's God, and I will exalt him. - Exodus 15:2

My son's heart and mind and soul have been restored to his Father. The flag has been planted, the territory captured. Love has won.

I have been crucified with Christ and I no longer live, but Christ lives in me. The life I now live in the body, I live by faith in the Son of God, who loved me and gave himself for me. - Galatians 2:20

Describe the relationship you would like to have with
God from this day forward.

_____
_____
_____
_____
_____
_____
_____
_____
_____
_____
_____
_____
_____
_____
_____
_____
_____
_____
_____
_____
_____
_____
_____
_____
_____
_____
_____
_____

PRAYER

Father,

Your love has won. In the battle for me, Your son, and the battle for my heart, mind, and soul – love has won. All this time I have walked in bondage, separated from You. But now I have turned back to You, have seeked You and called out to You, and I have found You.

I call on the perfect name of Jesus Christ and ask to live fully in Him. I ask to exist fully in His saving work of redemption and to remove the distance between me and my Father. I ask for this gap to be bridged so that I might restore our relationship to what it was intended to be.

I lay down my old self – all habits and worries and fear – I lay them all down at Your feet and look forward to continuing rebirth. I desire to be a new creation, restored from the inside out, and ask for the strength to battle against the enemy of my soul. I look to You as my source of all things. You are the provider of all that is good, and I will thank You for every daily blessing.

Fully restore my heart, mind, and soul, Lord. They are Yours. I present myself as a captive to You, God, and to Your plan for my life. Your love has won, Father.

Amen.

DAY 30

RETURNED FROM BATTLE

Dearest Son,

So you have returned from battle.

You are physically, emotionally, mentally, and spiritually spent. You are exhausted. You are bloody. You are filthy. And you are free.

Then you will know the truth, and the truth will set you free. - John 8:32

The territory that was once lost has been re-taken. The flag of Christ has been planted once again, and flies in glory over that most sacred place. I send my word to you - *well done, my son.*

For the Lord God is a sun and shield; the Lord bestows favor and honor; no good thing does he withhold from those whose walk is blameless. - Psalm 84:11

Celebrate this great victory with your brothers, but know that the attacks will continue. The sacred ground has been reclaimed, but has not lost any of its value. The enemy still desires it above all else. But you now stand equipped and ready for battle.

127

Cover yourself in armor.

The weapons we fight with are not the weapons of the world. On the contrary, they have divine power to demolish strongholds. - 2 Corinthians 10:4

Lock arms with your loved ones.

As iron sharpens iron, so one man sharpens another. - Psalm 27:17

Don't stop fighting. Fight for yourself and fight for your family. Defend your heart, that sacred ground, and do so in My name. You are worth it.

Be alert and of sober mind. Your enemy the devil prowls around like a roaring lion looking for someone to devour. Resist him, standing firm in the faith, because you know that the family of believers throughout the world is undergoing the same kind of sufferings. - 1 Peter 5:8

Well done, My son.

Set aside time today to read and think over your journey through this book. Describe your new understanding of who you are, and of what God wants for you.

_____

_____

_____

_____

_____

_____

_____

_____

_____

_____

_____

_____

_____

_____

_____

_____

_____

_____

_____

_____

_____

_____

_____

_____

_____

_____

PRAYER

Father,

You have brought me through to victory. You have broken the bondage that I walked in for so long. You have set me free. You have restored the pieces of my heart that were scattered, and You have transformed me through the renewing of my mind.

The presence of the enemy has been cast out. The territory of my heart and mind has been reclaimed in the name of Jesus Christ. I will now step fully into Your light, and follow it as I become the son, husband, and father that You created me to be. I will look to come closer to You at all times. I will pursue Your design for marriage with all the energy that I have. I will commit to raising my children in the way You have designed for it to be done.

I am claiming the freedom that You have bought for me, Father. I am asking for open eyes so that I can see everything You have for me. I am asking for open ears to hear all that You have to say to me. Cover me in Your armor, and let me stay next to You as I go into battle each day.

Because of You, I am free. Now allow me to use my freedom in a powerful way, Lord. Let me do the most that I can with my time here, Father.

Amen.

Dearest Son

ABOUT THE AUTHOR

Jeremy Lane is a writer living in North Texas with his wife and three children.

His work has been featured in many literary sites and journals, including MUSCADINE LINES: A SOUTHERN JOURNAL.

Jeremy's first collection of fiction, entitled *While I'm Still Myself*, was published in paperback by Tate Publishing early in 2012. A second collection, entitled *Everything Beautiful*, is being released in late 2015.

www.jeremymarklane.com

53208484R00079

Made in the USA
San Bernardino, CA
09 September 2017